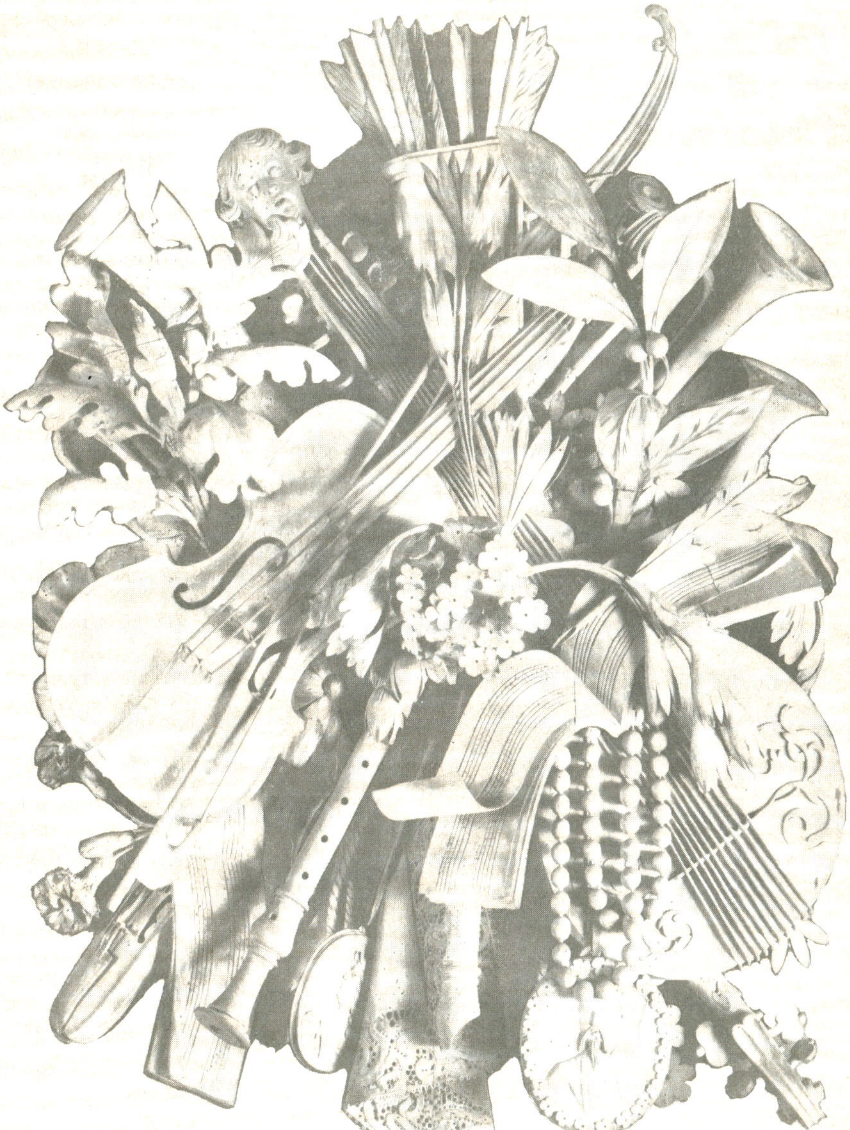

Dan & Erika,
   With many thanks for guide to Chicago and journal of your travels through Yugoslavia. You can sight-see by proxy among the British stately homes!
                                John

THE COUNTRY LIFE
PICTURE BOOK OF
COUNTRY HOUSES

BELVOIR CASTLE, LEICESTERSHIRE. The apeothesis of early 19th-century taste.

THE COUNTRY LIFE
PICTURE BOOK OF
COUNTRY HOUSES

COADE STONE PLAQUE AT BELMONT, KENT

COUNTRY LIFE LIMITED LONDON

First published in 1963
by Country Life Limited
2–10 Tavistock Street London WC2
Printed in Great Britain by
Robert MacLehose & Co. Ltd
Glasgow
© *Country Life Ltd* 1963

PUBLISHER'S NOTE

Many of the houses illustrated are open to the public, but by no means all of them. Care should, therefore, be taken before deciding to visit any of them. Full details may be found in *Country Houses Open to the Public* (Country Life, 8s. 6d.).

PREFACE

There are many histories of the English Country House. Some are weighty tomes and others short pictorial histories. This is neither: it is purely a picture book. The 106 photographs have been chosen for their pictorial as well as their architectural interest. The choice is a personal one and although the photographs are roughly in the chronological order of the houses, they have been arranged to make comparisons and contrasts that I find interesting, appealing or attractive. Because of its scale there are many noble absentees from the book, but these I hope to include in later selections.

JOHN CORNFORTH

LIST OF HOUSES AND OWNERS

Frontispiece: Belvoir Castle, Leicestershire (*Duke of Rutland*)
1 Warwick Castle, Warwick (*Earl of Warwick*)
2 and 3 Stokesay Castle, Shropshire (*Lady Magnus-Allcroft*) and Cothay Manor, Somerset (*Mrs Vera Astley-Rushton*)
4 and 5 Penshurst Place, Kent (*Viscount de L'Isle, V.C.*)
6 Penshurst Place (*Viscount de L'Isle, V.C.*)
7 Haddon Hall, Derbyshire (*Duke of Rutland*)
8 Herstmonceux Castle, Sussex (*Royal Greenwich Observatory*)
9 and 10 East Barsham Manor, Norfolk (*Colonel Anderson Wilson*) and Little Moreton Hall, Cheshire (*National Trust*).
11 Rufford Old Hall, Lancashire (*National Trust*)
12 Eltham Palace, London (*Crown Property*)
13 Montacute, Somerset (*National Trust*)
14 Longleat, Wiltshire (*Marquess of Bath*)
15 Burghley House, Northamptonshire (*Marquess of Exeter*)
16 Knole, Kent (*National Trust*)
17 Hatfield House, Hertfordshire (*Marquess of Salisbury*)
18 and 19 Burton Agnes, Yorkshire (*Mr Marcus Wickham-Boynton*)
20 and 21 The Vyne, Hampshire (*National Trust*) and Wilton House, Wiltshire (*Earl of Pembroke*)
22 and 23 Groombridge Place, Kent (*Mr S. W. Mountain*)
24 Sudbury Hall, Derbyshire (*Lord Vernon*)
25 Sudbury Hall, Derbyshire (*Lord Vernon*)
26 Ham House, Surrey (*National Trust*)
27 Ham House, Surrey (*National Trust*)
28 and 29 Petworth House, Sussex (*National Trust*) and Denham Place, Buckinghamshire (*Lady Vansittart*)
30 Ramsbury Manor, Wiltshire (*Lord Rootes*)
31 Winslow Hall, Buckinghamshire (*Mr and Mrs Edward Tomkins*)
32 and 33 Dyrham Park, Gloucestershire (*National Trust*) and Easton Neston, Northamptonshire (*Lord Hesketh*)
34 and 35 Blenheim Palace, Oxfordshire (*Duke of Marlborough*) and Grimsthorpe Castle, Lincolnshire (*Earl of Ancaster*)
36 Finchcocks, Kent (*Legat School*)
37 Barnsley Park, Gloucestershire (*Lord Faringdon*)
38 and 39 Ebberston Hall, Yorkshire (*Mr and Mrs de Wend Fenton*)
40 Houghton Hall, Norfolk (*Marquess of Cholmondeley*)
41 Holkham, Norfolk (*Earl of Leicester*)
42 Holkham, Norfolk (*Earl of Leicester*)
43 and 44 Baggrave Hall, Leicestershire (*Sir George Earle*)
45 Wentworth Woodhouse, Yorkshire (*Earl Fitzwilliam's Wentworth Estates Co.*)
46 Woburn Abbey, Bedfordshire (*Duke of Bedford*)
47 Ragley Hall, Warwickshire (*Marquess of Hertford*)
48 Uppark, Sussex (*National Trust*)

49   Uppark, Sussex (*National Trust*)
50   Badminton, Gloucestershire (*Duke of Beaufort*)
51   Althorp, Northamptonshire (*Earl Spencer*)
52   Woburn Abbey, Bedfordshire (*Duke of Bedford*)
53   Glynde Place, Sussex (*Mrs Humphrey Brand*)
54   The Vyne, Hampshire (*National Trust*)
55   Shugborough, Staffordshire (*The Trustees of the Earl of Lichfield*)
56   Corsham Court, Wiltshire (*Lord Methuen*)
57   Ince Blundell Hall, Lancashire (*Augustinian Canonesses Regular*)
58 and 59   Uppark, Sussex (*National Trust*) and Ombersley Court, Worcestershire (*Lord Sandys*)
60 and 61   Hagley Hall, Worcestershire (*Viscount Cobham*)
62   Claydon House, Buckinghamshire (*National Trust*)
63, 64 and 65   Claydon House, Buckinghamshire (*National Trust*), Gateley Hall, Norfolk (*Mr C. G. Hoare*) and Arbury Hall, Warwickshire (*Mr F. H. Fitzroy Newdegate*)
66   Donnington Grove, Berkshire (*Formerly The Hon. Mrs Reginald Fellowes*)
67   Malmesbury House, Salisbury (*Mrs Blenman-Bull*)
68   Syon House, Middlesex (*Duke of Northumberland*)
69   Osterley Park, Middlesex (*National Trust*)
70   Newby Hall, Yorkshire (*Major Compton*)
71 and 72   Newby Hall, Yorkshire (*Major Compton*)
73   Cranbury Park, Hampshire (*Mrs N. Chamberlayne-Macdonald*)
74   Osterley Park, Middlesex (*National Trust*)
75   Woburn Abbey, Bedfordshire (*Duke of Bedford*)
76   Heveningham Hall, Suffolk (*Hon. Andrew Vanneck*)
77 and 78   Heveningham Hall, Suffolk (*Hon. Andrew Vanneck*).
79   Heveningham Hall, Suffolk (*Hon. Andrew Vanneck*)

80   Wardour Castle, Wiltshire (*Cranborne Chase School*)
81 and 82   Moor Place, Much Hadham, Hertfordshire (*Mr R. C. Norman*) and Aynhoe Park, Oxfordshire (*Mutual Households Association Ltd*)
83   Belvoir Castle, Leicestershire (*Duke of Rutland*)
84   Belvoir Castle, Leicestershire (*Duke of Rutland*)
85   Belvoir Castle, Leicestershire (*Duke of Rutland*)
86 and 87   Belsay Castle, Northumberland (*Sir Stephen Middleton*)
88   Shrublands Park, Suffolk (*Captain the Hon. J. V. B. Saumarez*)
89 and 90   Rudding Park, Yorkshire (*Captain Everard Radcliffe*) and Horsted Place, Sussex (*Mrs Bouchard*)
91 and 92   Sezincote, Gloucestershire (*Mr C. A. Kleinwort*) and Harlaxton Manor, Lincolnshire (*Society of Jesus*)
93   Scarisbrick Hall, Lancashire (*St Katharine's (C.E.) College*)
94   Waddesdon Manor, Buckinghamshire (*National Trust*)
95   Sheringham Hall, Norfolk (*Mr Thomas Upcher*)
96   Mar Lodge, Inverness-shire (*Mr G. S. and Mr J. B. Panchaud*)
97   Castell Coch, Glamorgan (*Ministry of Works*)
98   The Red House, Bexleyheath, Kent (*Mr and Mrs Hollanby; Mr and Mrs Macdonald*)
99   The Wood House, Epping, Essex (*Essex Mica Co. Ltd.*)
100 and 101   Clouds, Wiltshire (*Church of England Children's Society*) and Knowsley Hall, Lancashire (*Earl of Derby*)
102   Flete, Devon (*Mutual Householders Association Ltd*)
103 and 104   Castle Drogo, Devon (*Mr Basil Drewe, Q.C.*) and Gledstone Hall, Yorkshire (*Lady Nelson*)
105   Mottisfont Abbey, Hampshire (*National Trust*)

INTRODUCTION

by Christopher Hussey

A good many of the million or so people who yearly visit historic houses are likely to enjoy this book, because it aims at presenting the aspects which most of us, whether inexpert or habitual viewers, chiefly look for and want to recall : the characteristic impression, the revealing detail, the telling comparison. While the photographs selected by Mr John Cornforth include many famous places and are arranged roughly in historical sequence, many have a refreshing slant, a little off beat.

The hundreds of houses now open to the public, and the much increased numbers who visit them, leave no doubt that the interest they arouse is much better informed than it was even ten years ago. Visitors compare one house with another, noticing significant details no less than period character. The growth in the cult of the historic house certainly justifies the limited measures taken by the government for their preservation : indeed warrants the more generous policy advocated when the existing legislation was being considered.

The very widespread appreciation shown of these houses' aesthetic, historical and architectural value substantiates the evidence presented at that time to the committee appointed by the Chancellor of the Exchequer. 'No country can rival', it was then stated, 'in number and beauty the English country houses in their familiar setting of gardens, avenues and park-lands. They are part of the English heritage, an association of beauty, art, and nature achieved through centuries of effort, which has seldom if ever been equalled in the history of civilisation. The English country house is the greatest contribution made by England to the visual arts. Reflecting some six centuries of our social history and domestic life, they remain a living element in the social fabric, showing in unbroken sequence how the planning, construction and adornment of the English home was adapted to changing conditions, social, economic, political and technical, to fresh aesthetic ideals and to new intellectual outlooks'. (Report of the Committee on *Houses of Outstanding Historical and Architectural Interest*, 1950.)

Something of a new intellectual outlook colours this book. Speaking as an old hand at introducing houses to people, what I like particularly about Mr Cornforth's way is its catholicity. For the first time, I think, in a general introduction of this kind, the nineteenth century is well represented. Instead of looking back across a gulf of a hundred and fifty years during which, it was implied, nothing of interest or value was produced, the sequence is brought down to the very edge of today. A gulf still intervenes ; but it has the merit of being much narrower, and being real. Houses of these kinds will never be built again. The representing of Victorian and Edwardian tastes has a further rather curious effect : their catholic values are subtly slanting our own, so that we appreciate the work of the old-established periods from a slightly different angle. It is this, perhaps, that helps to give the present book its freshness.

BEFORE THE DAYS OF THE ENGLISH COUNTRY HOUSE. The display of arms in the armoury at Warwick Castle. Within this beautifully situated castle, mainly of the 14th and 15th centuries, are splendid Stuart state rooms.

2 and 3. THE BEGINNINGS. Stokesay Castle, Shropshire, where the south tower was added in 1291 to the 13th-century Great Hall and Solar; and Cothay, Somerset, a remarkably complete manor house built about 1480 by a member of the Bluett family and redecorated about 1600.

4 and 5. SIX HUNDRED YEARS OF GROWTH: PENSHURST PLACE, KENT.

The hall range was built in the middle of the 14th century. Edward VI granted it to the Sidney family and Sir Philip Sidney was born there in 1554.

The position of the house near the church is typically English. From the 17th to the 19th centuries the head of a family occupied the big house, while a younger brother might be rector of the family living.

6. THE GREAT HALL AT PENSHURST. This was built by John de Poultney, Lord Mayor of London, about 1340. The interior retains its central hearth and carved timber roof.

A FORTIFIED MANOR HOUSE IN DERBYSHIRE: HADDON HALL. From 1170 to 1603 different generations of the Vernons added to and altered it as the pleasures of comfort replaced the needs of defence. The elopement of Dorothy Vernon from the house in 1567 brought it to the Manners family, later Earls and Dukes of Rutland.

A ROMANTIC BUT HOLLOW DISPLAY OF STRENGTH. By 1450, when Herstmonceux in Sussex was built, the age of medieval castle building was over. It was the earliest great house built of brick in the south of England. It was gutted in 1777, but was restored between 1913 and 1935. It now houses the Royal Greenwich Observatory.

9 and 10. NORFOLK BRICK-WORK AND CHESHIRE WOOD-WORK. East Barsham Manor, Norfolk, built about 1520–30 by Sir Henry Fermor, and Little Moreton Hall, Cheshire, built about 1559. These two houses stress in their materials the regional differences of English architecture.

1. THE GREAT HALL AT RUFFORD, LANCASHIRE. Rufford Old Hall was built about 1500 by Thomas Hesketh. The movable screen is a rare survival and there is also a remarkable hammer-beam roof.

12. THE INDIAN SUMMER OF THE GREAT HALL: ELTHAM PALACE, LONDON. It belonged to the Crown after 1311, but the hall was built in the reign of Edward IV. This photograph shows it as it was in 1927.

THE ELIZABETHAN VERNACULAR TRADITION: MONTACUTE, SOMERSET. It was built fifteen years after Longleat (Plate 14) was completed and shows little sign of the new manner.

14. THE FIRST FLOWER OF THE ENGLISH RENAISSANCE: LONGLEAT, WILTSHIRE. The house was built betwe[en] 1540 and 1580 by Sir John Thynne, who directed a succession of designers. The symmetry of the elevations is remarkable. The house [is] set in a superb landscape park.

15. ELIZABETHAN FANTASY AND DISPLAY: THE ROOF AT BURGHLEY HOUSE, NORTHAMPTONSHIRE. T[he] castles on the balustrades and chimneys are the crest of William Cecil, Lord Burghley, Queen Elizabeth's minister, who built the hou[se] between about 1553 and 1587.

THE GREAT STAIRCASE AT KNOLE, KENT. This early 17th-century staircase was inserted by Thomas Sackville, 1st Earl of Dorset, when he transformed the medieval house that once had belonged to the Archbishops of Canterbury.

17. JACOBEAN GRANDEUR: THE HALL AT HATFIELD HOUSE, HERTFORDSHIRE. The house was built between 1607 and 1612 for Robert Cecil, 1st Earl of Salisbury, under the direction of Robert Lyminge.

18 and 19. THE ELIZABETHAN STYLE MATURED: BURTON AGNES, YORKSHIRE. This house was built between 1600 and 1610 for Sir Henry Griffith by an unknown designer. The gatehouse stands at the entrance to the forecourt on the south front of the house.

20 and 21. THE BIRTH OF CLASSICISM IN ENGLAND. The South Front of The Vyne, Hampshire. The portico erected in 1654 was the first one built onto an English House.

The South Front of Wilton House, Wiltshire, built about 1647 to the design of Inigo Jones. The rooms are the most splendid surviving monument to the taste of Charles I's Court.

and 23. THE MODEST DIGNITY OF THE CAROLINE MANNER AT ITS BEST. Groombridge Place, Kent, built about 1660 by Philip Packer, a friend of John Evelyn, the diarist.

24. JACOBEAN AND CAROLINE DISPLAY AT SUDBURY HALL, DERBYSHIRE. Begun about 1613, the house was comple[ted] between 1660 and 1690. The Baroque centrepiece was added in this period.

5. THE RICHNESS OF CHARLES II DECORATION. The staircase at Sudbury Hall, carved by Edward Pierce in 1676, was carried out in a period of brilliant and spirited woodcarving and plasterwork.

26. THE BLUE DRAWING ROOM AT HAM HOUSE, SURREY. This remarkable house, built and decorated on various occasions in the 17th century, gives a vivid picture of the development of Stuart taste. The room seen here was decorated for the Duchess of Lauderdale in the 1670s.

'YE PICTURE CLOSETT': THE MINIATURE ROOM AT HAM HOUSE. This richly decorated little room and its contents have changed little since 1679, when an inventory was made of the house. The ceiling was painted about 1637 by Francis Cleyn.

28 and 29. THE GOLDEN AGE OF CRAFTSMANSHIP. A detail of the limewood carving at Petworth House, Sussex, by Grinling Gibbons, the greatest of the late-17th century carvers. A musical trophy in plaster on the ceiling of the saloon at Denham Place, Buckinghamshire It was modelled by an unknown plasterer at the end of the 17th century.

THE CAROLINE ACHIEVEMENT: RAMSBURY, WILTSHIRE. This was built about 1680–83 by Sir William Jones. It is based on the double pile plan worked out by Sir Roger Pratt in the 1650s.

A CHRISTOPHER WREN HOUSE: WINSLOW, BUCKINGHAMSHIRE. It was built about 1700 for William Lowndes, Secretary to the Treasury. This house and Fawley Court, Buckinghamshire, are the only two houses that can confidently be attributed to the designer of St. Paul's Cathedral.

32 and 33. THE BAROQUE SCALE. Examples by William Talman at Dyrham Park, Gloucestershire, and by Nicholas Hawksmoor at Easton Neston, Northamptonshire. These are among the principal surviving works of these two architects (elsewhere Hawksmoor appears as Vanbrugh's collaborator).

34 and 35. ARCHITECTURE FOR HEROES. Blenheim Palace, Oxfordshire, from the air, and the Great Hall, at Grimsthorpe Castle, Lincolnshire. Blenheim was designed for the Duke of Marlborough and Grimsthorpe for the 1st and 2nd Dukes of Ancaster by Sir John Vanbrugh, a playwright whose turn to architecture in middle life has never been satisfactorily explained.

36. THE BAROQUE ANGLICISED: FINCHCOCKS, KENT. This house was built in 1725 by Edward Bathhurst. The façade displays the influence of Thomas Archer.

DECORATION IN THE HALL AT BARNSLEY PARK, GLOUCESTERSHIRE. The elaborate plasterwork is attributed to Charles Stanley. The house was begun in 1720–21, but not completed until 1731.

38 and 39. THE VILLA INTRODUCED. Ebberston Hall, Yorkshire, was designed by Colen Campbell in 1718 and Chiswick House, Middlesex, designed by Lord Burlington in 1726.

THE STONE HALL AT HOUGHTON HALL, NORFOLK. One of the imposing state rooms created by William Kent for Sir Robert Walpole between 1722 and 1732.

41. THE PALLADIAN GRANDEUR OF THE MARBLE HALL AT HOLKHAM, NORFOLK. William Kent began this ho[use] in 1734 for Thomas Coke. Behind the sober front lies this hall modelled on the plan of a Roman basilica.

2. THE ROMAN DIGNITY OF THE STATE DINING ROOM AT HOLKHAM. William Kent's Palladianism in its most architectural mood. He was landscape gardener as well as architect.

43 and 44. THE EXCELLENCE OF GEORGIAN PROVINCIAL WORK: BAGGRAVE HALL, LEICESTERSHIRE The house was built in the 1750s for John Edwyn, High Sheriff of Leicester, by an unknown architect. It contain attractive plasterwork and woodwork.

45. ARISTOCRATIC SPREAD AT WENTWORTH WOODHOUSE, YORKSHIRE. The East Front is two hundred yards long and was designed by Henry Flitcroft in 1734 for the 1st Marquess of Rockingham.

THE GEORGIAN IDEAL: WOBURN ABBEY, BEDFORDSHIRE. The West Front, seen across the Octagon Pond, assumed its present form when it was rebuilt for the 4th Duke of Bedford by Henry Flitcroft.

47. PLASTERERS' PERFORMANCE: THE HALL AT RAGLEY HALL, WARWICKSHIRE. This was designed by James Gibbs about 1725 and further enrichments were made about 1755, possibly by Vassali.

GEORGIAN CIVILITY: THE DRAWING ROOM AT UPPARK, SUSSEX. It was built about 1700 by Sir Matthew Fetherstonhaugh; its original flock paper and decoration date from 1754.

49. THE SALOON AT UPPARK. This was decorated about 1770. The original white paint has a bluish tinge due to the high proportion of white lead; the gilding is original and so are the ivory silk brocade curtains.

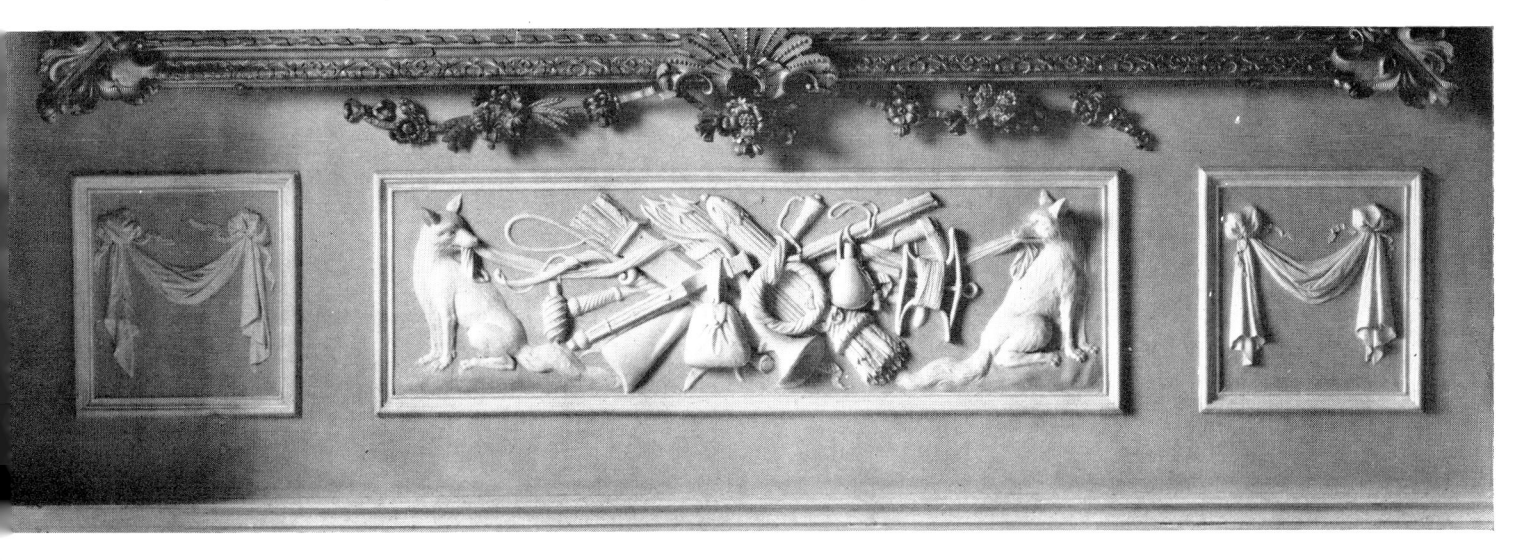

40. THE ENGLISHMAN'S LOVE OF SPORT. A detail of the plasterwork at Badminton, Gloucestershire.
In the following pages an attempt is made to suggest the effect of sport and other interests on the Georgian country house.

41. PAINTINGS OF HORSES. In the Hall at Althorp, Northamptonshire, there hangs a series of portraits of horses by John Wootton painted for the Earl of Sunderland in 1733.

52. STABLES ON A NOBLE SCALE AT WOBURN ABBEY. Between the two quadrangles built by Henry Flitcroft in 175? stands the Riding House, now demolished, built by Henry Holland in 1790.

53. THE GEORGIAN STABLES AT GLYNDE PLACE, SUSSEX. They are framed by two piers bearing the Trevor crest, th? Wyvern, and were built in the 1750s for Bishop Richard Trevor by John Morris, of Lewes.

54. AMATEUR ARCHITECTS. Architecture was studied by Georgian aristocrats, among whom were many talented amateurs, including Lord Burlington and John Chute, Horace Walpole's friend, who designed this staircase in 1765 for his Hampshire seat, The Vyne.

55. THE LIBRARY AT SHUGBOROUGH. Thomas Anson of Shugborough, Staffordshire, commissioned 'Athenian' Stuart to design his Library about 1762. Anson's interests extended to architecture and gardening as well as to books and coins.

56. THE PICTURE GALLERY AT CORSHAM COURT, WILTSHIRE. An early 18th-century collection of pictures is displayed in the setting designed for them by 'Capability' Brown in 1762. The new carpet was woven in Spain to reflect the ceiling design.

57. A DILETTANTE'S COLLECTION OF SCULPTURE. Henry Blundell displayed his collections made about 1777 and 1800 in this Pantheon built in 1802–10 at Ince Blundell Hall, Lancashire. The sculpture has been given to Liverpool Corporation.

8. A TASTE FOR PRINTS.
Among the many interests and
enthusiasms of the 18th century
was a taste for prints and for
decorating rooms with them as
in this dressing room at
Uppark, Sussex.

9. THE CHINESE
INFLUENCE. A long-lived
fashion was for Chinese rooms
of which this one at Ombersley
Court, Worcestershire, is a late
and elegant Regency example.

60 and 61. HAGLEY HALL, WORCESTERSHIRE. It was built between 1753 and 1759 by Lord Lyttelton, among whose friends were Sanderson Miller and John Chute, both amateur architects. The exterior, no longer strictly Palladian, is by Miller and its sober south front does not prepare one for the gay Rococo plasterwork of the hall within.

2. THE FANTASY AND VIRTUOSITY OF ROCOCO DECORATION. Part of the North Hall at Claydon House, Buckinghamshire, erected by Ralph Verney between 1752 and 1790. Florence Nightingale was a frequent visitor, for her sister was a Lady Verney.

63, 64, 65. THE IMAGINATION OF ROCOCO PLASTERWORK. A doorcase in the Chinese Room at Claydon; a detail of decoration done about 1750 in the hall at Gateley Hall, Norfolk; *(right)* part of the Saloon ceiling at Arbury Hall, Warwickshire, about 1786.

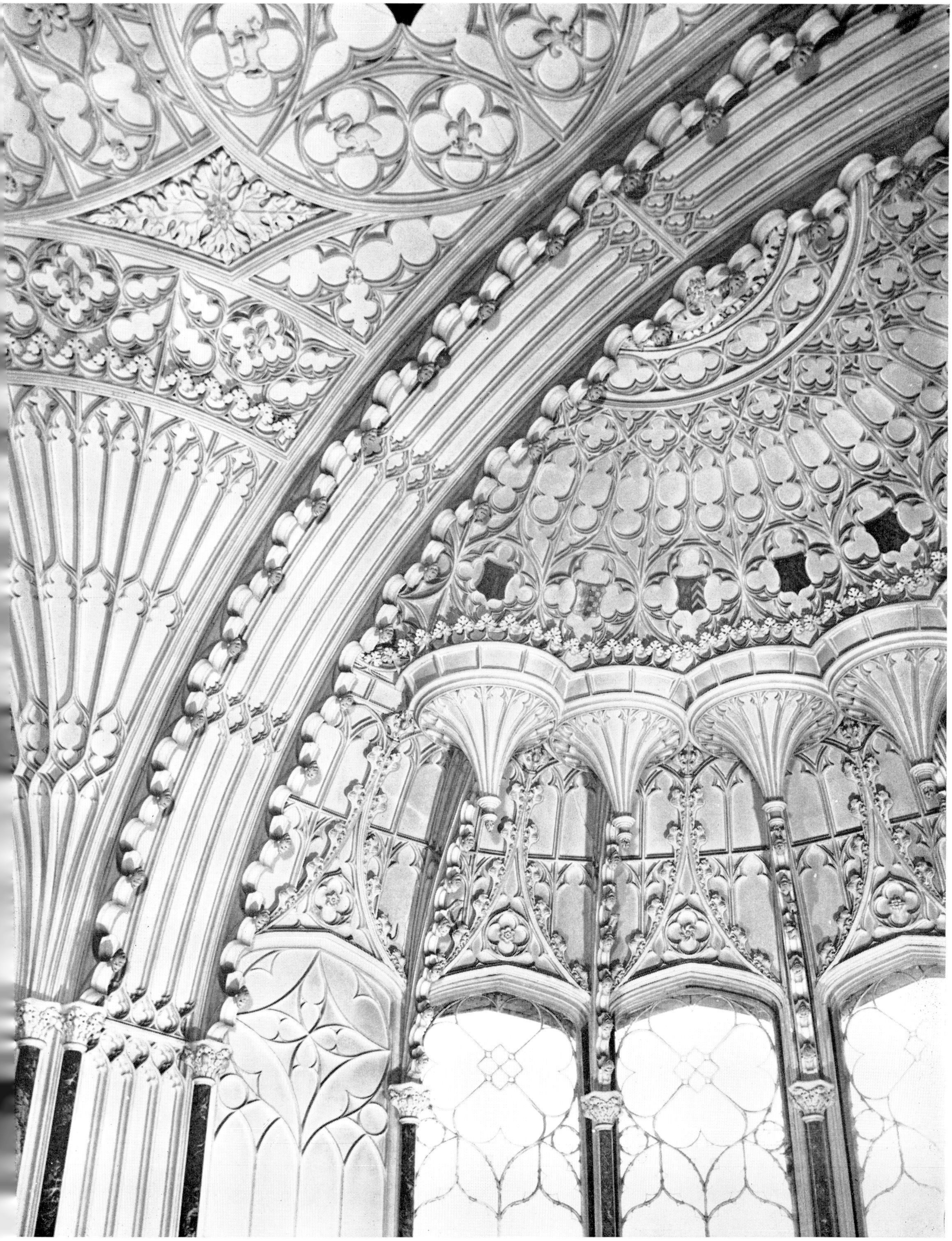

66. A GOTHICK VILLA: DONNINGTON GROVE, BERKSHIRE. It was designed about 1760 probably by John Chute and enlarged about 1785 by William Brummell, father of the 'Beau'

67. THE GOTHICK LIBRARY AT MALMESBURY HOUSE, SALISBURY. It was fitted up for James Harris, a man of letters, some time before 1750 a few years before Horace Walpole decorated Strawberry Hill in the Gothic taste.

ROBERT ADAM'S ROMAN MANNER: THE HALL AT SYON HOUSE, MIDDLESEX. It was decorated in 1762 and was the first of a magnificent set of state rooms done for the 1st Duke of Northumberland.

69. THE ENTRANCE FRONT AT OSTERLEY PARK, MIDDLESEX. Although more successful as a decorator of interi
Adam could employ such brilliant ideas as this portico cutting through the fabric of the old Tudor house.

70. NEWBY HALL, YORKSHIRE. The house was built about 1705 for Sir Edward Blackett. The wing on the right was adde
Robert Adam to contain the sculpture gallery shown in 71.

and 72. **THE SCULPTURE GALLERY AND THE ENTRANCE HALL OF NEWBY.** Both these were designed by Robert Adam for William Weddell, a great collector of sculpture. His alterations were carried out between 1767 and 1776.

73. THE BALLROOM AT CRANBURY PARK, HAMPSHIRE. The high standards of design and execution set by Adam we[re] maintained by his successors, who at times produced such masterly designs as this room done by George Dance the younger about 178[0].

THE TAPESTRY ROOM AT OSTERLEY, MIDDLESEX. Decorated by Adam in 1776, it is hung with Gobelins tapestries designed by Neilson after Boucher's *Les Amours des Dieux*. Another set with a different colour scheme hangs at Newby Hall.

75. HENRY HOLLAND'S LIBRARY AT WOBURN ABBEY, BEDFORDSHIRE. This room was formed when Holland rebu[ilt] the south range for the 5th Duke of Bedford after 1787.

JAMES WYATT'S ANSWER TO ADAM'S CHALLENGE. The Hall at Heveningham Hall, Suffolk. The rebuilding of the house for Sir Gerard Vanneck was begun in 1778 by Sir Robert Taylor and completed by James Wyatt before 1784.

77 and 78. THE ETRUSCAN ROOM AND THE LIBRARY AT HEVENINGHAM. The Etruscan Room is pale green with white mouldings and Etruscan red figures. The Library is also pale green and white, but the reliefs are set against brown purple, the colour of the porphyry columns and chimneypiece.

THE EPITOME OF NEO-CLASSICAL ELEGANCE AND REFINEMENT. The Saloon at Heveningham, painted by Biagio Rebecca in *trompe l'oeil*; the reliefs are in shades of green on a biscuit ground.

80. AN ENGLISH PANTHEON: THE GRAND STAIRCASE AT WARDOUR CASTLE, WILTSHIRE. It was designed James Paine, who built the house for the 8th Lord Arundell of Wardour between 1768 and 1776.

and 82. ARCS AND
CHES. Moor Place, Much
dham, Hertfordshire,
igned by Robert Mitchell;
Sir John Soane's Drawing
om at Aynhoe Park,
fordshire, formerly the seat
he Cartwright family.

83. **THE AGE OF LE ROI SOLEIL REVIVED.** The Elizabeth Saloon at Belvoir Castle, Leicestershire, about 18
An enthusiasm for French decoration was only one aspect of early 19th-century taste.

THE CASTLE IDEAL, AS REALISED AT BELVOIR BETWEEN 1800 AND 1825. James Wyatt was largely responsible for the Romantic silhouette that was desired by the 5th Duke of Rutland and his wife.

85. DUCAL GOTHIC: THE GUARDROOM AT BELVOIR. The interior of the castle was designed in a variety of styles from Norman and Gothic to French and Chinese.

and 87. GREEK NOBILITY: BELSAY CASTLE, NORTHUMBERLAND. It was built between 1807 and 1817 by Sir Charles Monck, who spent his honeymoon studying Hellenic architecture. The plan and the detailing of the house are inspired by Greek originals.

88. THE WINTER GARDEN AT SHRUBLANDS PARK, SUFFOLK. Winter Gardens were built in a number of styles from Indian Tudor Gothic and are one of the most attractive features of early 19th-century houses.

89 and 90. CLASSICAL OR TUDOR? THE WORLD OF THE WYATTS AND OF PUGIN. Half a century separates the elegant and practical design of Rudding Park, Yorkshire, begun in 1807, and the elaborately detailed Horsted Place, Sussex, built to the designs of Samuel Daukes in 1850–51.

91 and 92. THE EXTRAVAGANCE OF ROMANTICISM. In the search for novelty it was not considered too far-fetched to bedeck Sezincote in Gloucestershire in pseudo-Indian dress. The Elizabethan style was more popular and in the hands of Anthony Salvin and William Burn such a spectacular pile as Harlaxton Manor, Lincolnshire, was created between 1831 and 1855.

3 and 94. VICTORIAN GOTHIC AND THE CHATEAU STYLE. A. W. N. Pugin and his son, Edward, transformed and extended Scarisbrick Hall, Lancashire, between 1837 and 1870 in their rich and personal Gothic styles. Baron Ferdinand de Rothschild preferred the Loire chateaux style for his treasure house at Waddesdon, Buckinghamshire, built between 1874 and 1889.

95. EARLY VICTORIAN COMFORT: THE LIVING ROOM AT SHERINGHAM HALL, NORFOLK. The concept of an informal room was a new one when this room was finished in 1839.

96. THE EFFECT OF GENTLEMEN'S TASTE AND PLEASURES. This is the billiard room at Mar Lodge, Inverness-shire, built by the Duke of Fife in 1895–98.

7. CASTELL COCH, GLAMORGAN. The washstand in Lady Bute's bedroom, designed by John Chapple in 1891. The ruined medieval castle was restored for the 3rd Marquess of Bute by William Burges.

98. THE REVOLT OF WILLIAM MORRIS. He built the Red House at Bexleyheath, Kent, for himself and moved into it in 1860. It expresses his romantic longing for what he thought were the true values of the medieval world.

99. HOME OF A VICTORIAN CONNOISSEUR: THE WOOD HOUSE, EPPING, ESSEX. Built in 1893 and decorated to the designs of W. E. Tower and C. E. Kempe; the exterior was inspired by Sparrow's House, a 17th-century house in Ipswich.

100 and 101. ASPECTS OF VICTORIAN TASTE. The Morning Room at Clouds, in Wiltshire, begun by Philip Webb in 1880; and the Drawing Room at Knowsley Hall, Lancashire, photographed at the beginning of this century.

102. LATE VICTORIAN ROMANTICISM. R. Norman Shaw's Castle at Flete in Devon, which he began to construct round the old house in 1878 for Mr H. B. Mildmay.

3 and 104. THE LAST PHASE OF THE ENGLISH COUNTRY HOUSE? Probably time will prove that Sir Edwin Lutyens as not only the last but the greatest of the English Country House architects. Castle Drogo, Devon, and Gledstone Hall, Yorkshire, represent two manners of that eclectic master and also two recurring demands of English patrons.

105. IN THE TRADITION OF DECORATIVE PAINTING. A detail of the Drawing Room at Mottisfont Abbey, Hampshi[re] decorated by Rex Whistler in 1938–39. This talented artist was killed in Normandy leading his company soon after D-Day in 1944.

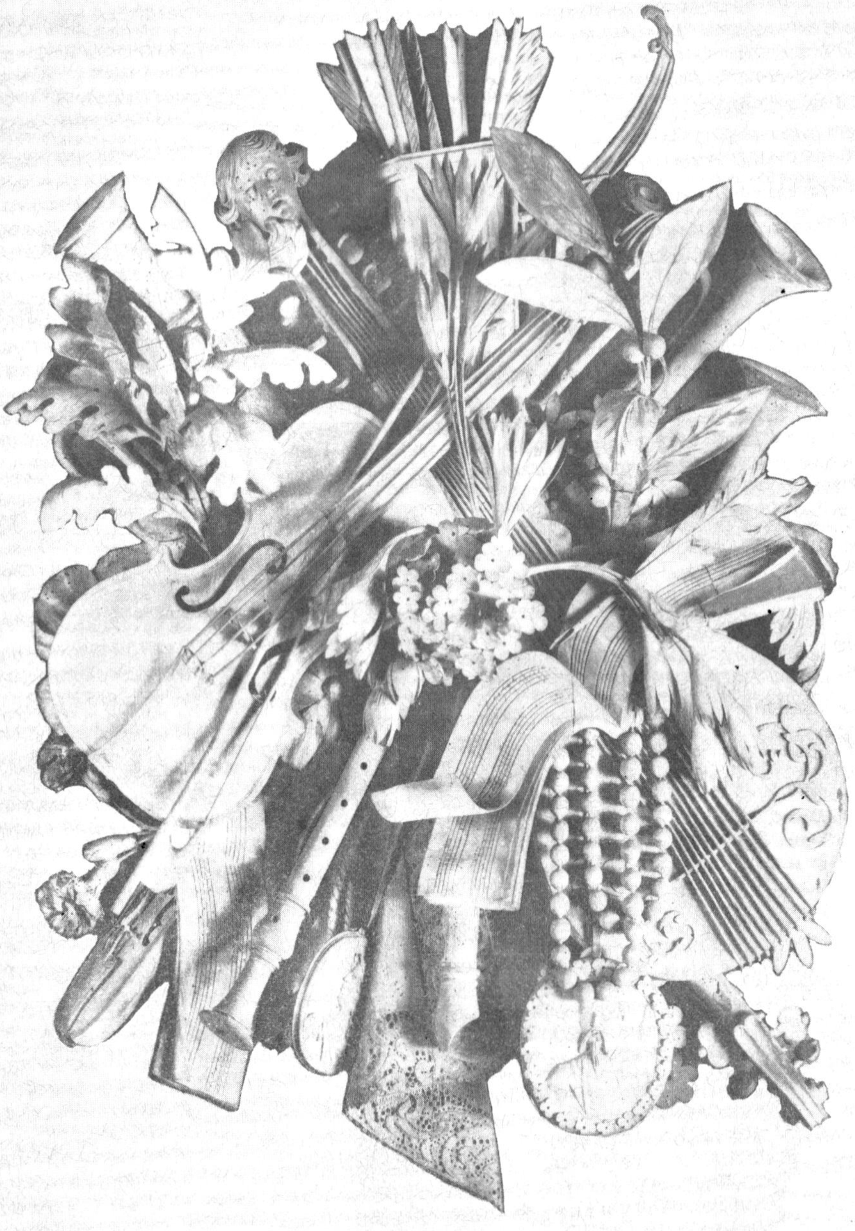